FIRST PET

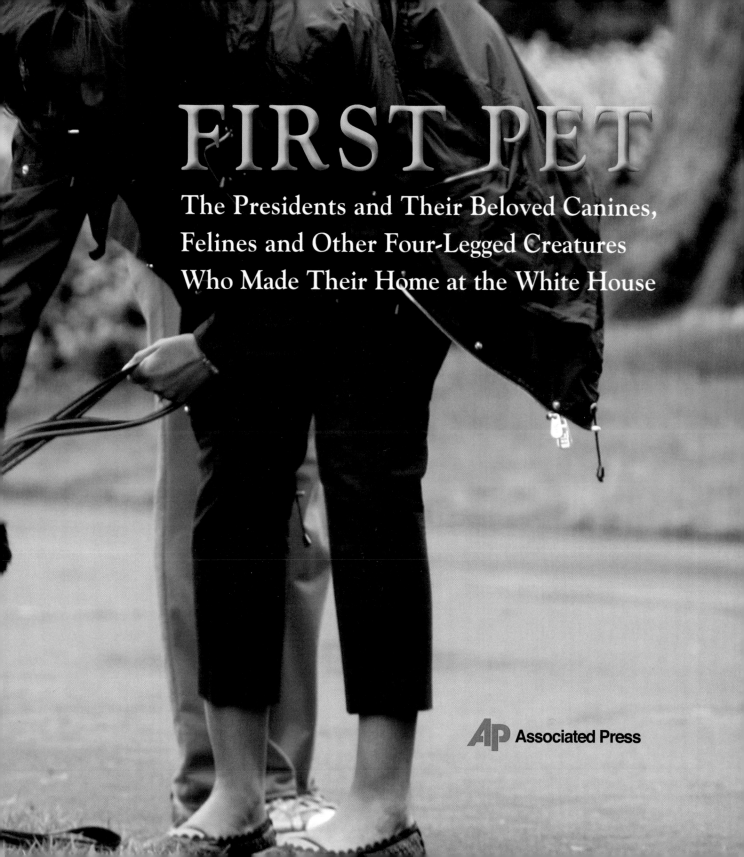

FIRST PET

The Presidents and Their Beloved Canines,
Felines and Other Four-Legged Creatures
Who Made Their Home at the White House

AP Associated Press

First Pet © 2010 by Associated Press
All rights reserved
Printed in the United States of America

Associated Press
450 West 33rd Street
New York, NY 10001

Library of Congress Control Number: 2010900871
ISBN: 978-0-9841927-0-0

Cover and book design by Bob Antler, Antler Designworks

Manufacturing by R.R. Donnelley

First Edition: 2010

10 9 8 7 6 5 4 3 2 1

Cover: *Bo, Portuguese water dog of the
Obama family, June 2009.* Half-title page:
*Socks, the cat of President Bill Clinton,
March 1994.* Pages 2-3: *President Barack
Obama, first lady Michelle Obama and new
dog Bo on White House lawn, April 2009.*
Page 4-5: *Mrs. Jacqueline Kennedy and
daughter Caroline ride a sleigh pulled by
Macaroni, pony of Caroline, on White House
grounds, February 1962.*

Contents

From the Publisher

THE ASSOCIATED PRESS

The Associated Press has reported on the White House and its inhabitants—both two-legged and four-legged—nearly since the foundation of the cooperative in 1846. AP correspondent Lawrence Gobright and President Abraham Lincoln even roamed the Capitol grounds together on horseback.

When AP launched its wire-service photography, the first family naturally became the subject of AP photographers. And, naturally, so did the first family's pets, some of which became household names and national characters in their own right. The photos in this book were drawn primarily from the decades of work produced by AP photographers, images preserved in the files of AP's voluminous photo library, and its online photo archive of more than seven million images on a multitude of topics. Some of the photos here are justifiably famous; others have been tucked out of sight for many years or never before seen. Virtually all are part of an unrivaled collection of presidential photography, with a depth and range of images that enable AP to offer this unique and remarkable body of work.

First Pet is the first of a new line of books being published under the imprint of the Associated Press. These exciting books reflect the rich tapestry of subjects captured by AP photographers worldwide and now come to life on these pages. The books of the Associated Press are published to entertain, inform, celebrate, and illuminate the world in which we all live, work, and play.

Left: President Calvin Coolidge and his wife Grace pose with sons Calvin Jr., left, and John, and one of the family's white collies, at the White House, June 1924. Above: Louis D. Boccardi, president of the Associated Press, meets with President Bill Clinton and first puppy Buddy in the Oval Office, January 13, 1998, as the news cooperative began the observance of its 150th anniversary.

Preface

This book is an exciting and rich photographic record of the presidents and their pets. Every one of the ten dozen or so photographs either entertains, educates, or informs us about the presidents and their relationships with their pet. And many of these extraordinary snapshots go deeper. They reveal something new or unique, or evoke a strong human emotion, such as in the photograph depicting the pure joy that the presidential duet of Lyndon Johnson and his dog Yuki were experiencing when they howled to the rooftops one of their favorite melodies.

From the very beginning of the American republic, animals—both domestic and wild—have been part of the presidency. Horses, bears, sheep, goats, dogs, cats, raccoons, and even hummingbirds have taken up residence at 1600 Pennsylvania Avenue. Those that didn't, such as the grizzlies, elephants, lions, and tigers that arrived as gifts from foreign leaders, were given to zoos or museums where, away from the whirling events of the presidency and the roaming lenses of the photographers assigned to cover them, they could be enjoyed up front and close by all Americans. Those pets that stayed at the White House and enjoyed the run of its grounds make up the subject matter of this book.

Among all presidential animals (and a few birds and reptiles), horses were prevalent prior to the twentieth century (all presidents owned some); but since, dogs have been by far the most common presidential pets. Barack Obama, the nation's forty-fourth president, has chosen Bo, a black-haired Portuguese water dog, as the family pet. Readers will find Bo among those featured and celebrated on the following pages.

This book is not for partisans or political junkies but rather for all animal lovers and history buffs, especially those who follow and celebrate the lives of American presidents and their families. The treatment is not intended as a comprehensive

Above: President Barack Obama's family dog Bo goes for a walk on the lawn in front of the White House in Washington in July 2009. Right: First lady Grace Coolidge displays her pet raccoon Rebecca to children gathered on the White House grounds for an Easter egg rolling, April 1927. Rebecca was one of two raccoons—the other was named Horace—that the Coolidge family kept as pets.

documentation in words and pictures. Rather, it is a treatment designed to lead the reader down memory lane as one might experience looking at a family album. In this case, the album's photographs are focused first on the pets and secondly their masters.

Just as a sage once mused, "You cannot collect all the beautiful shells on the beach," our book cannot include all the great photographs of the more than four hundred animals that have been presidential pets. However, the photos that we've selected stood out, so much so that they could not be overlooked.

So, turn the page and look them over.

Introduction

By CLAIRE McLEAN
FOUNDER AND DIRECTOR, PRESIDENTIAL PET MUSEUM

The number four hundred is close to the many animals and other creatures that crept, crawled, plodded, padded, or hoofed their way into the history of the White House and the presidency. Nearly all of these creatures, great and small, made a little history of their own. Some reached fame and fortune. Others were more pop- ular than their illustrious masters. Many were sent promptly to zoos, farms, or friends, and others, as gifts, were returned. The memorable ones found a niche in the history books and, through their eyes, tell a story about our presidents' inner instincts and even moments in the history of our nation. And nearly every one of these animals gives us more

to remember about the presidents and their families and, in doing so, enriches our national heritage.

How could one not be amazed at the importance of Fala, FDR's ubiquitous black Scottie? Or not enthralled by the story of Checkers, Vice President Richard Nixon's pet cocker spaniel, and his heartwarming journey from a donor in Texas to the Nixon family in Washington?

Or not mesmerized by the evocative campaign photograph of King Tut, Herbert Hoover's police dog, standing on two legs alongside Hoover with paws in his master's hands, bathing Hoover's austere and reserved personality with

Above: *U.S. President Herbert C. Hoover and first lady Lou Henry Hoover enjoy their vacation in August 1932 at Rapidan Camp, Virginia with their Norwegian Elkhound, Weeji. Right: First lady Barbara Bush, her granddaughter Barbara and Millie wait on the steps of the White House for President Bush to return from his check-up at Bethesda Naval Hospital in September 1991.*

warmth and sensitivity? Or not astonished at Millie, George and Barbara Bush's Springer spaniel, who "wrote" a best-selling book that outsold her master's memoirs?

If you doubt that White House pets have a powerful impact on the public, consider that the American Kennel Club's surges in breed registration closely track the types of breeds in the White House. Today,

President Barack Obama tries to keep up with six-month-old Portuguese water dog Bo (full name Bo Diddley), the family's new pet—a gift from the late Sen. Ted Kennedy, as first lady Michelle Obama and daughters Malia and Sasha follow behind on the South Lawn at the White House in April 2009.

the number of registered Portuguese water dogs is rising. Nearly a century ago, Warren Harding's Laddie Boy, an Airedale terrier, spurred the popularity of the breed and inspired the country's newsboys to chip in pennies to have a copper statue cast of this beloved

pet. Laddie Boy, whose statue is on exhibit at the Smithsonian Institute in our capital, is said to have had a better disposition than his master.

In the 1990s the public was amused by President Clinton's fiercely independent cat, Socks, and his running feud with Buddy, the Clintons' Labrador retriever. More recently, we were kept in suspense over the media's reporting of Obama's selection of

Left: Chelsea Clinton's cat Socks draws the attention of news photographers. Below: President Bill Clinton attempts to introduce his dog Buddy to Socks after returning from a visit to the Department of Education in January 1998. The meeting didn't go well. Socks rebuffed Buddy, who soon retreated to the safety of the Oval Office.

Left: Laddie Boy, the pet Airedale terrier of President Warren G. Harding, greets the president at the entrance to the White House as the president returns from a trip to Florida in 1923. Laddie Boy was accustomed to the frequent absences of his master and would sit quietly while waiting for the president's return. Ever alert, he would spring to his feet whenever an automobile would turn through the White House gates.

Bo, the first pet currently in the White House. Up close and personal news stories that feature the presidents and his pets make our presidents—on balance—more beloved by the public.

Our presidents show goodness of heart during their private and personal moments with the animals with which they have bonded. Bill Clinton took solace in Buddy, his chocolate Labrador retriever, during trying impeachment days; George W. Bush noted that only his dogs, Springer spaniel Spot and Scottish terrier Barney, were there to comfort him during a choking episode.

President Andrew Jackson showed his soft nature by writing to his new daughter-in-law Sarah, proclaiming that "a dog is

Left: *First puppy Buddy greets President Bill Clinton in March 1998, upon the president's return to the White House.* Right: *President George W. Bush plays with his dogs Barney (in front of the president) and Spot (behind) on the grounds of the White House. Spot is the son of Millie, the family pet of President George H.W. Bush.*

one of the most affectionate of all the animal species and is worthy of regard, and Andrew's [his son] attachments for his dog is an evidence of the goodness of his heart."

Woodrow Wilson, who was dogless most but not all of his life, is said to have pronounced, "If a dog will not come to you after he has looked you in the face, you might go home and examine your conscience."

Harry Truman is credited with having said that "if you want a friend in Washington, get a dog," and yet he is known to have given away the sweet yellow cocker spaniel named Feller, a surprise gift from a woman in Missouri, to White House physician Brigadier General Wallace Graham. This disturbed the dog-loving public. Truman did see the error of his ways, though, and allowed his daughter Margaret to let her Irish setter, Mike, reside at the White House—though he too was moved out of the White House for health reasons.

Virtually all of our presidents knew the value of animals and birds, wild and domestic, in their presidencies, and while Chester A. Arthur escapes our scrutiny, every other commander has had a pet, a favorite riding or driving horse, or enacted legislation benefiting wildlife. For example, Millard Fillmore, while not having a pet about the White House, was one of the founding members and president of the Buffalo ASPCA. Much credit is given to his interest in caring for neglected animals.

George Washington, at Mount Vernon, was the leader in presidential animal husbandry as he recorded more than thirty hounds and other animals that he used as breeding and hunting stock. The animal inventory at Mount Vernon at one time reached over 150. Washington's interest in hounds, briards, wolfhounds, turkeys, geese, mules, and other critters was formidable.

Thomas Jefferson wanted to populate America with "the most careful, intelligent dogs in the world" and chose the French briard by placing some with nearby landowners. He is said to have instituted the first dog license by asking all dog owners to collar their animals

First lady Grace Coolidge with Rob Roy, a white collie, and Paul Pry, an Airedale terrier, accompanying children at the White House Easter egg roll, April 1925. The Coolidges had eleven dogs, many of which had colorful names such as Boston Beans, a bulldog, Calamity Jane, a white collie, and a bird dog named Palo Alto.

The Clinton White House's first feline, Socks, paws and claws around in the arms of first lady Hillary Rodham Clinton during an East Room event in February 1999 introducing her new book featuring Socks and Buddy, the president's Labrador retriever. The book includes children's letters to the first pets and a short history of animals that have roamed the White House in the past.

and to be responsible for their mischief.

The list of our presidents' animals started modestly with the hounds of Washington and the briards of Jefferson, but it grew quickly, counting the horses of the earlier presidents, the gifts from dignitaries, the personal pets of each president, the ménage of Abraham Lincoln (including the first litter of cats), and Calvin Coolidge's impressive family of domestic, exotic, and wild animals. Many wild animals such as lion cubs, a wallaby, a pygmy hippo, and a bear were added to the National Zoo by Theodore Roosevelt and his large family, and again by Grace and Calvin Coolidge.

The large presidential pet menageries of Coolidge and Roosevelt were exceptions, and today not as many animals reside at the White House. But the importance of their presence in the political scene is just as important now as it has been in the past. Don't you think Woodrow Wilson's sheep grazing on the White House lawn sent a perfect message to the public about the war effort? While today there may be no sheep on the south lawn and fewer pets per president, a product of our time, their impact—especially in the image-making arena of politics—should not be underestimated.

In 1992 Bill Clinton was "cat"-a-pulted into the White House, but by his second term he came to see the advantage in courting the dog-loving public. During Clinton's 1996 presidential campaign against Republican Bob Dole, a *Time* magazine Paw Poll reported that Dole's schnauzer, aptly named Leader, outpolled Socks the cat by 51.1 percent even though the dog didn't have a chance to unseat the

President Bill Clinton walks Buddy, his chocolate Labrador retriever as first lady Hillary Rodham Clinton and daughter Chelsea make their way across the White House grounds in August 1998 on their return from vacation at Martha's Vineyard, Massachusetts. Buddy is the only Labrador retriever ever to roam the White House grounds as a presidential pet.

cat. It may have led to Buddy, a chocolate Labrador retriever, joining Bill, Hillary, and Chelsea in 1997, shortly after Clinton's re-election. Perhaps Clinton was wisely taking heed of Calvin Coolidge's admonition, "Any man who does not like dogs, and does not want them about, does not deserve to be in the White House."

And so the stories and the tails go on. While pets are certainly not into politics, it is certain that presidents are into pets, and it is one similar interest that crosses all party lines and unites a common cause: the public's fascination with pets and the presidency. We are almost certain that the next president and the next will have the same desire to show warmth of character and acknowledgment of the human-animal bond by showing off his or her interest in, and affection for, the animal companions that share top-dog status in Washington, D.C.

This book, which touches upon the most prominent and perhaps a few heretofore obscure pets, shows us not only the joy of pet ownership but also the importance of responsible pet care and how this stewardship starts at the top, with the president of the United States. Most of all, *First Pet* explores that fabulous connection between pets and presidents, and showcases with its unique photographs a rich niche in American history that is very dear to our hearts.

Doggin' It

A PRESIDENT'S BEST FRIEND

If you want a friend in Washington, get a dog.

—President Harry Truman

Obama has his Bo. W. had Barney. Bill had Buddy. George H.W. Bush had Millie. Ronnie had Rex. Gerald Ford had Liberty. LBJ had Yuki.

In fact, it's been more than fifty years—since the presidency of Harry S. Truman (1945-1953)—that a dog has not had the complete run of the White House, providing companionship, adding luster to the presidency, or even making history as first pet.

Truman, who was not an animal lover, was the first president to publicly cast aside a first pet. He briefly owned a cocker spaniel named Feller, a gift arriving from a Missouri woman just before

Christmas 1947. When Truman gave the dog to his personal physician, dog lovers howled. In protest, they renamed the pup Feller the Unwanted Dog.

Left: *President George W. Bush's dog Barney enjoys the outdoors on the grounds of the White House in December 2004. Center/below: Feller, a five-week-old cocker spaniel puppy sent to President Harry Truman as a Christmas gift, poses beside his crate in a White House corridor on December 22, 1947. Right: President Bill Clinton is greeted by his dog Buddy as he returns to the White House in August 1998.*

Since then, no dogs have been so publicly banished from 1600 Pennsylvania Avenue, and only one other president, Lyndon B. Johnson (1963–1969) has run afoul of animal lovers, when he was criticized loudly for picking up one of his pet beagles by

Left: *President Gerald R. Ford sits with his dog Liberty, a golden retriever, in the Oval Office.* Center: *President George H.W. Bush walks across the White House lawn with his Springer spaniel Millie and five of her six puppies in 1989.* Right: *President Lyndon B. Johnson holds his dog Her by the ears as White House visitors look on. At left is President Johnson's other dog, Him. This picture raised criticism from dog lovers.*

Above: *President Franklin D. Roosevelt lifts his dog Fala while motoring to the yacht Potomac at New London, Connecticut, where he began a 10-day vacation voyage in August 1941.* Right: *President Barack Obama walks his six-month-old Portuguese water dog Bo on the White House grounds in April 2009.*

the ears. Overall, thirty-two presidents have welcomed canines into the White House as the official pet of the first family. Every president since Warren Harding (1921–1923), who had Laddie Boy, an Airedale, had at least one dog in the White House. Almost all of these best friends stayed on for the full terms of their respective masters and lived high-profile lives. The breeds of these presidential pets have ranged from bulldogs to spaniels to terriers to retrievers to hounds to Portuguese water dogs.

Some became nearly as famous as their masters. Millie, the Springer spaniel of President George H.W. Bush (1989–1993) and first lady Barbara, was the first dog to author a best-selling book, *Millie's Book: As Dictated to Barbara Bush*. The book gave

Fala, left, President Franklin D. Roosevelt's pet Scottie, joins her puppies Meggie and Peggie. The photograph was taken two days after FDR died in April, 1945. The names for the five-week-old puppies were suggested by the late President.

President Ronald Reagan muses with reporters and photographers in August 1981 after being taken by surprise by his faithful canine companion Millie, who lived at the president's California ranch near Santa Barbara. Millie joined her master shortly after the president completed signing landmark legislation cutting the federal budget and taxes.

readers a dog's-eye view of happenings in the White House. Millie also gave birth to Spot, the family pet of George W. Bush (2001–2009), our forty-third president and son of George and Barbara.

Barney, George W.'s good-natured, black Scottish terrier, became a star by way of the newest mass media outlet—the Internet. In a series of "Barney Cams" that appeared on YouTube, he shared the spotlight with a wide range of luminaries, from Karl Rove, the president's close political adviser, to British prime minister Tony Blair and singer Dolly Parton.

Fala, a Scottish terrier that

belonged to Franklin Delano Roosevelt (1933–1945), was a star from the moment he entered the White House in 1940. He was a gift from FDR's favorite cousin, Margaret Suckley, who later wrote a biography of Fala, *The True Story of Fala*.

Fala loved the limelight. The dog became as much an A-list celebrity as FDR, regularly appearing alongside the president in news photos of events in and out of the White House.

Wherever the president went Fala was

Sequence of Three Photos: *Jake, an Irish setter who lived at Congressional Country Club in nearby Potomac, Maryland, joins President Gerald Ford in his practice session on the golf range. Jake would lie down and watch until the president swung; then he would bound after the flying ball.* Right: *President George W. Bush walks with his dog Barney on his ranch in Crawford, Texas.*

sure to follow. He joined FDR for dinner each evening at 7 PM, attended the president's press conferences, rode to official ceremonies in the president's limousine, and even attended diplomatic summits such as FDR's meeting with Stalin at Yalta. In 1941 Fala accompanied FDR aboard the USS *Augusta* when FDR met with British Prime Minister Winston Churchill in the middle of the Atlantic Ocean for the leaders' signing of the Atlantic Charter.

The first presidential pet dog that gained national attention and celebrity status was Lara, a 170-pound New-

Above: *Future President Franklin Delano Roosevelt, 2, perches on a pet donkey with his dog Budgy in 1884.* Right: *President Franklin D. Roosevelt plays with his pet Scotch terrier Fala at the White House in 1943.*

foundland who was first dog of President James Buchanan (1857–1861). When Buchanan was inaugurated in 1857, the widely read *Frank Leslie's Illustrated Newspaper* (called *Leslie's Weekly*) ran an engraved illustration of Lara, predicting that the "dog will hereafter become historical as a resident of the White House."

Fido, the mongrel belonging to President Abraham Lincoln (1861–1865) and his family, was the first dog of a president in office to be photographed. The image was taken in the studio of F.W. Ingmire in Springfield, Illinois, just prior to Lincoln's inauguration in 1861. But the event proved bittersweet for the family. Concerned by the dog's aversion to the bewildering crescendo of sights and sounds of the political campaign, such as cannon blasts signaling the president's nomination, they left Fido behind in Springfield with close friends.

Tragically, Fido was also the first president's pet to die at the hands of a murderer. Less than a year after President Lincoln's assassination on April 14, 1865 by John Wilkes Booth, an enraged drunkard stabbed the dog to

President Bill Clinton holds three-month-old chocolate Labrador retriever Buddy, who at the time of this photograph—snapped in December 1997—was yet unnamed. After a half-hour tryout on the White House grounds the president decided to keep the dog. The president named the dog after his late great-uncle Henry Oren "Buddy" Grisham who had died earlier that year. Buddy died on January 2, 2002 in Chappaqua, New York, when struck by an automobile.

Above: *First pets Scottish terrier Barney, left, and Springer spaniel Spot, play on the White House grounds. Barney was a gift from New Jersey Governor Christine Todd Whitman. Spot is the offspring of former first dog Millie who was owned by first lady Barbara Bush. Right: President Lyndon Johnson lets his beagle Him peer from open window as the president toured Johnson City, Texas, in November 1965. Opposite page: President George W. Bush pets his Springer spaniel Spot, in the Oval Office.*

death on a street in Springfield. According to John Roll, whose family was taking care of Fido, the dog had made the fatal mistake of putting his dirty paws upon his attacker in a playful manner.

America's Roaring Twenties saw two astonishing firsts by presidential canine pets. Laddie Boy, first dog of Warren Harding (1921–1923), was the first dog to add his paw prints to the daily goings-on of government. Laddie Boy sat in on executive branch meetings, perched on his own hand-carved chair. He greeted official visitors to the White House on its front steps. President Harding created an exchange of letters in a national political magazine between Laddie Boy and a vaudeville dog named Tiger. Laddie Boy's response to a letter from Tiger provided a forum for the president to put forth a thinly veiled defense of Harding's swelling political scandals through Laddie Boy's stating that anyone can be undone by people who used friendship for personal gain. Even the *Washington Star* newspaper conducted mock interviews with Laddie Boy, eliciting his opinions on issues such as eight-hour days for watchdogs.

Left: *Republican presidential hopeful Herbert Hoover holds his pet dog King Tut in the photo that circulated widely during the 1928 presidential campaign. Some observers credited it with helping boost Hoover's image in his win over Democratic candidate Al Smith.* Above: *Republican vice-presidential nominee Richard Nixon plays with the family's black and white cocker spaniel Checkers at his Washington home in September 1952 following his famous TV/radio broadcast. Nixon had defended the gift of Checkers to his children from a Texas supporter, as well as a fund of some $18,000 that his supporters had publicly set up to allow him keep in touch with voters in his home state of California.*

However, it was police dog King Tut, first dog of Herbert Hoover (1929–1933), who was thrust prominently for the first time ever into a presidential campaign. Hoover's campaign managers discovered—and then exploited—a highly evocative photograph of the dog alongside the conservative Republican. The photograph, which combined a steadfast gaze of the dog's trustful eyes with candidate Hoover's benign and plaintive pose, communicated a warm "man loves his dog" message. Thousands of autographed pictures were circulated during the campaign, which helped Hoover defeat his opponent, Democrat Al Smith, by carrying forty of forty-eight states and garnering 58.2 percent of the popular vote. For the first time in a national election, a dog in a photograph may have helped to sweep a president into office.

Hoover was not the first president to use a dog for political gain. Andrew Jackson (1829–1837), a populist president who had country roots—he was born in a small cabin in South Carolina—populated the White House with hunting hounds and mixed breeds to remind the people of his humble background. William Henry Harrison (1841), our ninth president, who died from pneumonia after serving only one month in office, was the first to take his dog with him during the presidential campaign. Newspaper coverage often mentioned the dog, including one reporting that the dog of the hero of the battle of Tippecanoe welcomed the governor of Virginia "with a cordial and significant shake of his tail."

The most momentous event—likely the first and last time such an event will ever occur in presidential politics—of a dog swaying public opinion occurred not during a presidency but during Richard M. Nixon's ascendency to the office of vice president. In 1952, after Nixon was selected to run with Dwight D. Eisenhower

(1953–1961), he was forced to explain a fund of approximately $18,000 that was established by his supporters after he won his California senate seat; the money was raised to allow him to keep in touch with his Golden State constituents.

Nixon went on television, then a new mass medium, and used Checkers, the family dog, to appeal to the emotions of the audience. His following words, about the acquisition of Checkers, saved Nixon's career: "The day before we left on this campaign trip we got a message from Union Station in Baltimore saying they had a package for us. We went down to get it. You know what it was? It was a little cocker spaniel dog in a crate [sent by a man from Texas who knew the Nixon children wanted a dog]—black and white, spotted. And our little girl Tricia, the six-year-old, named it Checkers. And you know, the kids love the dog, and I just want to say this right now, that regardless of what they say about it, we're gonna keep it!"

Nixon, like most presidents and their families, enjoyed dogs as first pets for their companionship and playfulness. Nixon's

predecessor, Lyndon B. Johnson (1963–1969) took his mutt, Yuki, with him almost everywhere—from his Texas ranch to the White House pool to the signing of important legislation to his daughter Luci's wedding. LBJ also had two best friends in his beagles, Him and Her. He gave the beagles the run of the White House and carried treats for them in his pocket.

John F. Kennedy (1961–1963) found companionship in a Welsh terrier named Charlie. JFK swam with Charlie in the White House pool and played fetch with balls and the floating toys of his children, John and Caroline. Charlie brought not only play but also comfort to JFK. He was with the president during the early events of the Cuban missile crisis, calmly sitting on JFK's lap while the president stroked his back. Medical researchers have demonstrated that the simple act of petting a dog in times of stress will lower blood pressure, steady a heartbeat, and calm

Left: *Yuki, the white mixed breed first pet of President Lyndon Johnson goes airborne while accompanying his master and Colonel Frank C. Malone, commanding officer of Bergstrom Air Force Base in Texas as they stride from the presidential jet.* Below: *President Lyndon Johnson poses with Freckles, mother of five beagle pups, at the White House in November 1966. The father of the pups was Jones Brookline Buddy, owned by Jean Austin DuPont of Wilmington, Delaware.*

Left: *President Theodore Roosevelt reads in the doorway of a house in Colorado with his dog Skip on his lap in April 1905.* Above: *As Christmas draws near, the three White House pets—Pasha, Tricia's Yorkshire terrier, Vicki, Julie's silver poodle and King Timahoe, President Nixon's Irish setter, all of whom would be on hand for Christmas Day—sit before the first family's tree on the second floor of the executive mansion in December 1971.* Opposite: *General Dwight D. Eisenhower, Allied commander for North Africa, holds the leash of his Scottish terrier Caacie as he meets Navy Secretary Frank Knox at an airport in October 1943.*

one's nerves. Kudos to first pet Charlie, who did just that for JFK in a critical moment of our nation's history.

Long before he assumed the office of the presidency, Dwight D. Eisenhower (1953–1961) benefited from the companionship of a dog during a crisis, driving the Germans from North Africa in World War II. In 1943, General Eisenhower wrote his wife, Mamie, about Caacie, a Scottish terrier: "The friendship of a dog is precious. I have a Scottie. In him I find consolation and diversion. He is the 'one person' to whom I can talk without the conversation coming back to the war." When Ike moved to England to prepare the Allied invasion of Normandy on D-Day, he took

43

in Teddy's estimation, lived up to the saying, "It's not the size of the dog in the fight, it's the size of the fight in the dog." According to our twenty-sixth president, Skip was willing to stand his ground against menacing threats of bodily harm twenty times the little dog's height and weight, such as brown and black bears. Skip was a little dog ("a little of this and little of that," according to Teddy) with a heart as big as all outdoors, and everyone knows how much the leading Rough Rider of San Juan Hill loved America's open spaces.

Skip was a constant companion of Roosevelt. They rode together, Skip in front on the saddle. They read together, Skip on Teddy's lap, the president's book resting on the dog's back. Skip died one year before Teddy left office. He now rests in peace at the Roosevelt estate at Sagamore Hill in New York, where his master died in 1919, eleven years later.

Left: A "Beware of Dog!" sign hangs outside the Oval Office in March 1989, during the administration of President George H.W. Bush. Millie, the first family's pet Springer spaniel, was expecting puppies in about two weeks. Above: First dog Bo plays with a ball on the White House grounds. When Bo's primary walker, first lady Michelle Obama, is out of town, Dale Haney, Superintendent of the White House Grounds, can often be seen with Bo. "I have him a little bit more when she's traveling," said Haney. He is amazed by the public's fascination with White House pets: "Sometimes I think they're more interested in the pets than the president ."

Caacie, and when he moved into the White House ten years later he brought along another Scottish terrier, named Spunky.

Theodore Roosevelt (1901–1909) had several dogs, but his favorite was Skip, who was Teddy's companion and fellow hunter. Roosevelt loved the spirit and fight in the dog who,

George Washington (1789–1797) to James Buchanan (1857–1861)

According to one White House historian, the essence of our presidents and their pets is that "the pets were ordinary and their masters were not." Many presidents and other historians would likely quarrel with that observation. However, whether ordinary or extraordinary or a mix of both, the pets of American presidents have evolved through the more than 230 years of our democratic republic.

For one, the mix and choices of presidential pets have reflected the changing character and nature of American society, especially that of work. As the nation evolved, so did the pets of the president. Our many presidents and their first families loved their pets as much as Barack Obama's family loves Bo, their Portuguese water dog; but our early presidents, especially those of the eighteenth and nineteenth centuries, assigned multiple roles for their animals and pets, and in doing so, assessed their value differently. Following the customs of the day, they gave them many of the important chores and tasks of American daily living. Their pets were not just companions or animate showpieces. They were helpers, and they earned their keep.

Our early presidents lived in a predominately agrarian world in which the raising of animals and crops was widely practiced. Sheepdogs were popular, not so much because they were good companions or because the dog might project an image of a kinder, gentler chief executive, but because they could keep watch and control a president's flock of sheep, important livestock that provided food and clothing. Hounds, such as the foxhounds of George Washington and coonhounds of Andrew Jackson, helped to not only protect domestic animals by hunting and killing predators such as foxes, but also to bag and put wild game on the family table. No dogs—not even the early first dogs—had a free lunch.

For their amusement, early presidents kept the likes of canaries, hummingbirds, mockingbirds, and parrots, but they were not central to the chief executive's survival as were their working horses and dogs, grazing sheep, cattle and goats, and free-range turkeys and chickens. They kept riding horses, such as their wartime mounts, for personal transportation, and carriage horses for getting their families from place to place for special events and everyday visits.

Although President George Washington never resided in the White House (it was not completed until 1800), he kept wartime mounts, Blueskin and Nelson. The latter he triumphantly rode at Yorktown during the British surrender. Our first president kept his hunting horses and carriage horses in stables at the president's residences in the capital, located successively in New York City and Philadelphia, and at his Virginia home, Mount Vernon. His horses went on hunts. They pulled carriages. They walked trails. They trotted the byways and roads. They provided the primary means of overland transportation.

John Adams, our second president, recognized the need to house horses when he built the first White House stables on a parcel of ground just east of the eighteen acres that surround the White House. Thomas Jefferson abandoned the Adams stables, which were a bit removed from the White House, and built new

Andrew Jackson, seventh president of the United States, in an 1829 depiction, takes an extra horse with him as he starts off for his inauguration

ones closer, plus a carriage house and cowshed.

After the British destroyed these buildings in 1814, the horses of the presidents went several years in need of a permanent housing. This was finally realized during President Andrew Jackson's second term when he built a permanent structure in which he housed Sam Patches, his wartime mount, as well as several other Jackson horses, including Truxton, his champion racehorse which—not counting first lady Dolley Madison's talkative

parrot—could be considered the first celebrated presidential pet. The young nation had an extraordinary president and an extraordinary presidential pet in residence at the White House at the same time.

Jackson also kept and trained four racing fillies: Emily, Lady, Nashville, and Bolivia. Old Hickory, who loved thoroughbreds and loved racing them even more, found recreation and sport (and even derived wagering income) in his horses.

Old Whitey, the wartime mount of Zachary Taylor, also stayed in the stables upgraded by Jackson. However, Jeff Davis, the wartime mount of Ulysses S. Grant, enjoyed newer quarters in the stables built in 1871 by Uncle Sam (as President Grant was affectionately called).

Along with dogs that hunted and watched over domestic stock animals, horses—wartime mounts, riding horses, hunting horses, racing horses, carriage horses—were abundant among presidential pets in the early days of our republic and they got their shelter and oats the old-fashioned way. They earned them.

U.S. PRESIDENTS 1789–1861

George Washington

John Adams

Thomas Jefferson

James Madison

James Monroe

John Quincy Adams

Andrew Jacks...

1. George Washington (1789–1797)

Dogs: Hounds Mopsey, Taster, Cloe, Tipsy, Tipler, Forester, Captain, Lady Rover, Madame Moose, Sweetlips, and Searcher, and Vulcan, one of five French hounds given by his friend, the Marquis de Lafayette.

Horses: Among several stallions Samson, Steady, Leonidas, Traveller, Magnolia, his mounts during the Revolution, Nelson and Blueskin, a horse given by British General Edward Braddock, Rozinante, horse of granddaughter Nellie Custis.

Other: Parrot belonging to the first lady, Martha Washington.

2. John Adams (1797–1801)

Dogs: Two dogs of the first lady, Abigail Adams.

Horses: Cleopatra and others. He built the first White House stables.

3. Thomas Jefferson (1801–1809)

Dogs: Two briards, a gift from the Marquis de Lafayette.

Other: A mockingbird named Dicky among others, a pheasant, peacock, and two grizzly bears, a gift from explorer Zebulon Pike, in October 1807.

DID YOU KNOW? George Washington named a Maltese jackass, a gift from the Marquis de Lafayette, Knight of Malta.

4. James Madison (1809–1817)

Other: Green parrot that belonged to first lady Dolley Madison, sheep.

DID YOU KNOW? Dolley Madison's green parrot is said to have outlived both the president James and the first lady.

5. James Monroe (1817–1825)

Dogs: Sheepdogs and black spaniel belonging to granddaughter Maria Monroe.

DID YOU KNOW? Thomas Jefferson trained Dick, his mockingbird, to sing along as he played the violin.

6. John Quincy Adams (1825–1829)

Other: Alligator that visited for two months with its owner, the Marquis de Lafayette, silkworms raised by first lady Louisa Adams.

7. Andrew Jackson (1829–1837)

Dogs: Several hunting hounds and mixed breeds.

Horses: Wartime mount Sam Patches, racing fillies Emily, Lady Nashville, and Bolivia, champion racehorse Truxton, and ponies.

Martin Van Buren

William Henry Harrison

John Tyler

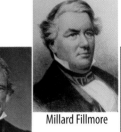

James Polk

Zachary Taylor

Millard Fillmore

Franklin Pierce

James Buchanan

Other: A parrot named Polly who screamed curse words at Jackson's funeral, and a gamecock.

8. Martin Van Buren (1837–1841)

Other: Two tigers, a gift of the sultan of Oman, which he gave to a zoo.

9. William Henry Harrison (1841)

Dogs: A mixed breed that campaigned with his master (who died after one month in office). Other: Durham cow named Suki and a billy goat.

> **DID YOU KNOW?**
> *Zachary Taylor proclaimed that his horse, Old Whitey, was smarter than most ordinary folk and all politicians.*

10. John Tyler (1841–1845)

Dogs: An Italian greyhound named Le Beau, a gift from the consul of Naples, two Italian wolfhounds imported for first lady Julia Tyler.

> **DID YOU KNOW?**
> *William Henry Harrison purchased a cow named Suki to provide dairy products for the White House.*

Horses: The General.
Other: The canary Johnny Ty, among others.

11. James Polk (1845–1849)

No known pets, but grew up riding horses.

12. Zachary Taylor (1849–1850)

Horses: His wartime mount, Old Whitey.

13. Millard Fillmore (1850–1853)

Other: Mason and Dixon, ponies.

14. Franklin Pierce (1853–1857)

Dogs: Seven Chinese Pekingese sleeve dogs, gifts from Commodore Matthew Perry. Pierce kept one, naming the dog Bonin, and gave another to Jefferson Davis, who later became president of the Confederacy.

15. James Buchanan (1857–1861)

Dogs: A Newfoundland, or "Newfie," named Lara.
Other: A pair of bald eagles.

THE FRENCH CONNECTION
THE MARQUIS AND HIS MAGNIFICENT HERDERS

Five of the first six United States presidents and their dogs had a French connection, or more specifically, a connection to the Marquis de Lafayette, the rebellious French aristocrat who came to America in defiance of his king to join the American Revolution. Presidents George Washington, Thomas Jefferson, James Madison, and James Monroe owned French breeds gifted by the Marquis, or in the case of John Quincy Adams, assisted Lafayette in delivering the dogs to America by accompanying them on board the transatlantic trip by ship.

In 1785 Lafayette gave Washington seven large French staghounds, which were known for their stamina and ability to concentrate when on the trail of a quarry. When Lafayette sent them to America he enlisted the aid of John Quincy Adams, who escorted the dogs to the port of New York.

Unfortunately, Adams was not much of a dog enthusiast. Upon arrival in New York, he abandoned the dogs to the care of the shipping company. Washington eventually located the dogs but not before expressing his disapproval: "It would have been civil in the young Gentleman to have penned me at least a note respecting the disposal of the [foxhounds]." Nevertheless, the dogs eventually arrived safely at Mount Vernon, and Washington began in earnest to fulfill his dream of developing an ideal foxhound for the New World.

Washington was more than a devoted breeder of hounds. He loved varying aspects of his dogs and greatly admired their hunting and tracking qualities. He loved the deep bellows of his new French dogs on the hunt, which he likened to "the bells of Moscow." He admired their speed and ability to swiftly cover open ground in the Virginia countryside. Our first president was our first chief executive dog lover as well.

His goal as a breeder was to create an enhanced hybrid that would complement his Virginia hounds, which he felt were too lightly built and lacking the strength for sustained hunts over the expansive Virginia countryside. Washington sought "a superior dog, one that had speed, scent and brains"—a new breed that had the tenacity and intelligence of the Virginia foxhound as well as the speed, power, and focus of the French staghounds.

Over a relatively short span of time Washington successfully mixed the two breeds, carefully combining the best, desired qualities of both. Several years later Washington's friends at the Gloucester Foxhunting Club in New Jersey crossed his new American foxhounds, which had been given to the club members while Washington attended the Continental Congress in Philadelphia, with some English foxhounds to give them a more traditional Old World look. It was more a cosmetic upgrade than a wholesale change in the character of the breed, one that did not dismantle Washington's efforts. To this day, Washington is generally acknowledged as the developer of the American foxhound, a breed that was larger and faster than the Virginia foxhound.

Thomas Jefferson was also the recipient of two dogs from Lafayette, as well as the progenitor of an American version of a very intelligent French sheepdog, the chien berger de Brie, also known as the briard, a breed that dates back to Charlemagne. In 1789 Jefferson sailed to America from France with his newly acquired (for $6 plus $1.50 tip) and very pregnant briard named Buzzy, who gave birth to two pups during the transatlantic crossing. Jefferson later received as a gift from Lafayette two more briards to serve as guardians of his sheep at Monticello.

Madison temporarily housed a pair of Jefferson's sheepdogs at his Montpelier estate in Virginia before giving them to a friend in Washington.

From July 1824 to August 1825 the Marquis de Lafayette, the Revolutionary War hero, journeyed from France to make a final tour of the United States. In July 1825, with an alligator in tow, he visited President John Quincy Adams and first lady Louisa at the White House.

Prior presidents had dotted the grounds of the White House with nearly all types of four-legged and feathered friends—horses, sheep, dogs, a jackass, mockingbirds, a peacock, a pheasant, and a couple of parrots—but Lafayette's representative of the reptilian world was the first to crawl its way around the grounds. For two months the alligator took up residence in the East Room of the White House. Its presence likely shortened the stays of many of the president's other summertime visitors. When Lafayette ended his visit, he took the alligator with him. It's not known if the alligator accompanied Lafayette on his return voyage to France but he did carry with him a barrel of American soil, which was eventually placed around his grave.

First lady Louisa Adams kept the smallest among all White House pets. She raised silkworms, feeding them mulberry leaves, and wound their silk, which was then sewn into gowns for the first lady. The silkworms—like so many other presidential pets in our nation's formative years— earned their keep.

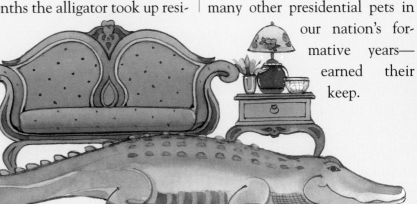

THREE RECORD-BREAKING PETS IN ONE WHITE HOUSE:
THE BIGGEST, THE MOST PATRIOTIC, AND (ALMOST) THE HEAVIEST

The biggest dog to take up residence in the White House was Lara, a 170-pound Newfoundland. President James Buchanan brought the dog with him to the White House from his Wheatland estate near Lancaster, Pennsylvania. White House staff and visitors alike observed Lara's unusual practice of lying motionless for hours with one eye open and one eye closed. As the nation's first bachelor president—his niece, Harriet Lane, acted as first lady—Buchanan greatly valued the dog's loyalty and companionship, especially since he was the only president to remain unmarried throughout his life. The dog and his master were truly best friends.

President Buchanan also owned a pair of bald eagles (the bird on the presidential seal). Their stay at the White House was short-lived. They were sent to Wheatland and took up residence on the back porch of the estate.

In 1861, during the waning days of Buchanan's administration, the king of Siam wrote to the president that he had heard that the United States had no elephants. As a remedy, and in a gesture of friendliness between the two countries, the king offered a gift of elephants—several pairs of them—that could be "turned loose in forests and increase till there be large herds."

36"
From floor to shoulder

Lara
170 lbs.
Newfoundland

7' From nose to tail

JEFFERSON'S GRIZZLY CUBS

He wrote, "The elephants would be useful in the unsettled parts of the United States since elephants being animals of great size and strength can bear burdens and travel through uncleared woods and matted jungles where no carriage and cart roads have yet been made."

Such an offer might have resonated with a nineteenth-century, visionary disciple of Hannibal—the legendary Carthaginian general who took his army to war on elephants weighing six tons each over the Pyrenees and Alps into Italy, but it gained little traction in Washington.

When the reply to this generous and extraordinary offer passed to President Buchanan's successor, Abraham Lincoln, Honest Abe politely declined the elephants, explaining that the geography and climate of the United States do not "favor the multiplication of the elephant."

In late October 1807, President Thomas Jefferson received two grizzly cubs—a male and female—as a gift from explorer Zebulon Pike, who had been exploring along the Arkansas River. Pike, who recognized that the grizzly was a different species of bear from that found in the eastern part of the United States, informed Jefferson in a letter announcing their imminent arrival: The grizzlies are "considered by the natives of that country [in the southern region of the great Continental Divide] as the most ferocious animals of the continent."

Jefferson had heard firsthand accounts of the western grizzly from Meriwether Lewis and William Clark when they briefed the president following their expedition to the Pacific. Jefferson made a quick decision, as documented in a letter to his granddaughter, Anne Cary Randolph, when he mentioned the arrival of the grizzly cubs from Pike: "These are too dangerous and troublesome for me to keep . . . I shall therefore send them to [Charles Willson] Peale's Museum."

It took nearly two months for the president and his staff to get the cubs on their way to Philadelphia, site of Peale's Museum, which had an abiding interest in exhibiting objects of natural history. While at the White House, the bears outgrew their original cage and were transferred to a new cage-like enclosure on the White House South Lawn where they could be seen by the public.

Jefferson's political opponents gleefully referred to this public display as the president's "bear-garden," a term going back to Elizabethan-era bear-baiting arenas and which still carried the negative connotation of a rough, noisy area that lacked decorum. It wasn't until January that Jefferson bade his final farewell to the grizzlies.

Abraham Lincoln (1861–1865) to Calvin Coolidge (1923–1929)

The transitioning of presidential stables into auto garages heralded a change in the roles of presidential pets, a change that's still in place today.

In 1909, the handsome stables built by President Grant were converted into a garage that housed both the elegant cars of President William H. Taft and his dairy cows, Mooly Wooly and Pauline Wayne. In 1911, they were torn down and replaced by a garage solely for housing automobiles, although through the late twentieth century, horses remained available to the White House at nearby army stables for recreational riding.

The number of presidential pets embodied as helpers and workers—that is, the dairy cows

Above: *Pauline Wayne, one of two pet cows (the other was named Mooly Wooly) of President William Howard Taft, grazes on the lawn in front of the State, War and Navy Building in Washington, D.C., between 1909 and 1913.* Right: *First lady Grace Coolidge plays with her white collie, Rob Roy, and her Airedale terrier, Paul Pry, in September 1924.*

(Taft's Pauline Wayne), hunting dogs (Washington's Vulcan and Teddy's Skip), and transportation-providing carriage horses (Grant's Egypt and St. Louis) and cart-pulling goats (Benjamin Harrison's Old Whiskers)— slipped significantly during the era of the presidency from Lincoln to Coolidge, 1861 to 1929. Distinctly different pets, including some exotics from abroad, joined the animal parade at the White House.

Cows, chickens, geese, sheep, turkey, goats, and other farm stock still inhabited the White House grounds but their roles were definitely shifting. They were now secondary to the White House's food-chain supply, except perhaps for one famous throwback: President Taft's cow, Pauline Wayne, who gave fresh milk each day for the president's afternoon snack.

Presidential pets became less functional. In fact, a pet's stock rose if he brought not only a work ethic but also playfulness, entertainment, and companionship to 1600 Pennsylvania Avenue. In some cases, our presidents welcomed pets that were not only entertainers but also curiosities. Benjamin Harrison kept two opossums named Mr. Reciprocity and Mr. Protection. William McKinley had a Mexican double yellow-headed parrot named Washington Post. Teddy Roosevelt kept a blue macaw named Eli Yale; Woodrow Wilson had Old Ike, a tobacco-chewing ram; and Calvin Coolidge kept— among a menagerie of animals

First lady Grace Coolidge holds the family's pet raccoon, Rebecca. The Coolidges also owned another raccoon, Horace, as well as several other wild animals as pets, including (if only briefly) a bobcat named Smokey.

President Warren G. Harding and first lady Florence Harding appear on a White House balcony with their pet Airedale terrier, Laddie Boy in 1923. Laddie Boy, who sat in his own chair at cabinet meetings, inspired the nation's newsboys to chip in pennies to have a copper statue cast of this beloved pet. The statue is on exhibit at the Smithsonian Institute in Washington.

Below: *A White House staffer tends to the dogs of President Warren G. Harding and his wife Florence on the White House lawn in 1921. At left is Oh Boy, a bulldog, with the president's Airedale terrier, Laddie Boy, at right.* Right: *first lady Grace Coolidge displays her pet raccoon Rebecca to children gathered on the White House grounds for an Easter egg rolling in April 1927.*

Laddie Boy, the pet Airedale terrier of President Warren G. Harding, gazes at a "radiotone" portrait of himself in silver, which was presented to first lady Florence Harding by Alfred H. Retler in July 1922. The first lady also owned a canary named Bob.

President Warren G. Harding plays with his pet Airedale terrier Laddie Boy outside the White House in June 1922. Right: President Calvin Coolidge stands with one of the family's collies on the steps of Patterson House in Washington D.C., in 1927. Patterson House, on Dupont Circle, was the first family's temporary residence while the White House was undergoing renovations in 1927.

and birds—a goose named Enoch and two raccoons named Rebecca and Horace.

Since the day that Washington swore his oath to defend the Constitution, presidential pets were gifts from foreign officials, and this era proved no different. They were, however, more distinctive and diverse. Presidents Rutherford B. Hayes, Grover Cleveland, William McKinley, and Theodore Roosevelt were among the presidents who added diversity—that is, foreign-sourced pets—to the expanding list of presidential pets.

President Hayes (1877–1881) introduced to America and the White House grounds the first Siamese cat, named Miss Pussy, a gift from the first lady of Siam. Presidents Cleveland (1885–1889 and 1893–1897) and Teddy Roosevelt each kept a Pekingese dog from China. The United States was a global power, and, among other indicators, a modest but noticeable international mix of presidential pets reflected its reach into far-flung places and nations.

16. Abraham Lincoln (1861–1865)

Dogs: Fido, family dog that stayed in Springfield, Jip, the president's dog, and others.

Other: Ponies belonging to Tad and Willie, Tad's goats Nanny and Nanko, Tad's turkey Jack, white rabbits, and cats.

17. Andrew Johnson (1865-1869)

Other: It is known that President Johnson during the time of his impeachment left flour out at night for a family of mice.

18. Ulysses S. Grant (1869–1877)

Dogs: Son Jesse's Newfoundland, Faithful.

Horses: His wartime mounts Jeff Davis, Cincinnatus, and Butcher Boy; saddle horses Egypt and St. Louis; carriage horses Jennie and Mary; Nellie Grant's mares.

Other: Shetland ponies Reb and Billy Button, parrot and gamecocks, belonging to Jesse.

DID YOU KNOW? *Ulysses S. Grant was arrested, and his horse and carriage impounded, for speeding on a Washington street.*

General Ulysses S. Grant, commander of the Union Army during the Civil War, poses with one of his wartime mounts. General Grant had three horses he rode in the Civil War: Jeff Davis, Cincinnatus and Butcher Boy. The date and location of this photograph are unknown.

19. Rutherford B. Hayes (1877–1881)

Dogs: A Newfoundland named Hector, an English mastiff named Duke, Scott's greyhound Grim, a cocker spaniel named Dot, and two hunting dogs named Shep and Juno.

Horses: Several carriage horses.

Other: Pedigreed Jersey cows, goat belonging to Scott, a mockingbird, four canaries, a pigeon, first lady Lucy

DID YOU KNOW? *Rutherford B. Hayes had his horse shot out from under him four times while fighting in the Union army during the Civil War.*

Left: *Grover Cleveland with his pet spaniel. Cleveland was the 22nd and 24th U.S. President, 1885-89 and 1893-97. Above: President Grover Cleveland is joined by a young boy and a spaniel.*

Left: *In the absence of President Warren Harding and first lady Florence Harding for the annual White House Easter egg roll, the first family's pet Airedale terrier Laddie Boy acted as host for the many children who rolled eggs on the White House lawn in April 1923.* Above: *First lady Grace Coolidge plays with Rob Roy, her beautiful, pure-white collie, on the White House south grounds.*

Hayes's cats Piccolomini and Miss Pussy—the first American Siamese cat, a gift from the first lady of Siam—and kittens.

20. James Garfield (1881)

Dogs: Veto.

Horses: Molly Garfield's mare named Kit.

Other: Fish.

21. Chester Alan Arthur (1881–1885)

No known pets.

22. Grover Cleveland (1885–1889)

Dogs: A dachshund, a spaniel, and Hector, first lady Frances Cleveland's Japanese poodle (or poochin, a mix of poodle and Japanese chin).

Other: Mockingbird and canaries.

23. Benjamin Harrison (1889–1893)

Dogs: Dash.

Horses: Abdullah, Lexington, Billy, and John.

Other: Billy goat named Old Whiskers, opossums named Mr. Reciprocity and Mr. Protection, and a bird.

24. Grover Cleveland (1893–1897)

See President Number 22.

25. William McKinley (1897–1901)

Other: Mexican double yellow-headed parrot named Washington Post. Mother and her four Angora kittens, including Valeriano Weyler, named after the governor of Cuba, and Enrique DeLome, namesake of the Spanish ambassador to the United States.

26. Theodore Roosevelt (1901–1909)

Dogs: Sailor Boy, a Chesapeake Bay retriever, Jack, a Manchester terrier belonging to son Kermit, Pete, a bull terrier, Manchu, a black Pekingese belonging to daughter Alice, and Skip, a mongrel.

Horses: Bleistein, Teddy's favorite horse among Renown, Roswell, Rusty, Jocko, Root, Grey Dawn, Wyoming, and Yagenka, plus carriage horses General and Judge.

President Calvin Coolidge and first lady Grace Coolidge are flanked by their hosts, Mr. and Mrs. Howard E. Coffin, in December 1928 as they make their way to the Coffin's Sapelo Island estate off the coast of Georgia. King Kole, the Coolidge's black Belgian police dog, rests in the president's arms.

Left: *Laddie Boy, the pet Airedale terrier of President Warren G. Harding, celebrates his third birthday with a birthday cake, July 25, 1922. Above: Photographer Edward S. Curtis, known for his photos of Native Americans and the American West, plays in the sand with young members of President Theodore Roosevelt's family as they partially bury one of their dogs at Sagamore Hill, the family home in Oyster Bay, N.Y., circa 1904. From left: President Roosevelt's sons, Quentin and Archie, Curtis, and Nicholas Roosevelt, a cousin of the president.*

Other: Algonquin, a calico pony of son Archie, a bear named Jonathan Edwards, lion, wildcat, coyote, zebra, lizard named Bill, rat named Jonathan, unnamed kangaroo rat, badger named Josiah, pig named Maude, several snakes including one named Emily Spinach belonging to Alice, a six-toed cat named Slippers and another named Tom Quartz, a flying squirrel, a rabbit named Peter, hyena, and several birds including a blue macaw named Eli Yale, a hen named Barong Spreckle, a barn owl, a one-legged rooster, an eagle, several parrots and canaries.

27. William Howard Taft (1909–1913)

Other: Two cows, Mooly Wooly and Pauline Wayne, the last cow to forage on the White House lawn.

28. Woodrow Wilson (1913–1921)

Other: Sheep, chicken, songbirds, Puffins the cat, and Old Ike, a tobacco-chewing ram.

29. Warren G. Harding (1921–1923)

Dogs: Laddie Boy, an Airedale that sat in his own chair at cabinet meetings, and Oh Boy, a bulldog.

Other: Turkeys and canaries, including one named Bob, belonging to first lady Florence Harding.

30. Calvin Coolidge (1923–1929)

Dogs: Peter Pan, a terrier, Paul Pry, an Airedale terrier, Rob Roy and Calamity Jane, white collies, chow chows named Tiny Tim and Blackberry, a brown collie named Ruby Rough, a bulldog named Boston Beans, a black Belgian police dog named King Kole, a yellow collie named Bessie, and a bird dog named Palo Alto.

Opposite and above: Laddie Boy, the pet Airedale terrier of President Warren G. Harding, poses with and without his master in undated photos.

Other: Cats Tiger, Bounder, and Blackie, a donkey named Ebenezer, a bobcat named Smokey, raccoons named Rebecca and Horace, a wallaby, a cow, two lion cubs— a gift from the mayor of Johannesburg, South Africa, mother and baby Pygmy hippos, a bear, an antelope, Nip and Tuck, Hartz Mountain olive-green canaries, Snowflake, a white canary, Enoch, a goose, Old Bill, a thrush, Goldie, a yellow bird, a mockingbird, mynah bird, parrot, and a flock of chickens.

Many presidents are bona-fide animal lovers, and several have built their menageries to prove it. By sheer volume, two presidents—Theodore Roosevelt and Calvin Coolidge—topped the list.

Teddy Roosevelt, his wife Edith, and six children populated the White House with more than forty pets. His favorite was a mongrel dog named Skip, whom the president found during a bear hunt in the Grand Canyon. Skip regularly joined the president when he took horseback hunting trips in the West, often riding on the president's saddle in order to keep pace with the riders. Skip also enjoyed napping on the president's lap while he read a book. He died in 1907, writing the final chapter to what Teddy called "a happy little life."

The many other dogs of the Roosevelt family included Sailor Boy, a Chesapeake Bay retriever who was known to swim behind the presidential yacht; Tip, his wife Edith's mongrel; and Mutt, another mongrel plucked from the local dog pound when Tip ran away; Rollo, a friendly St. Bernard; Manchu, a black Pekingese presented to daughter Alice Roosevelt by the Empress Dowager Ci-Xi of China; and the notorious bull terrier Pete, who was banished to Sagamore Hill, Teddy's summer house in New York State, after ripping the pants of French ambassador Jules Jusserand.

The Roosevelts kept several riding horses, among them Bleistein, Teddy's favorite; Renown, Roswell, Rusty, Jocko, Root, Grey Dawn, Wyoming, and Yangenka; and two carriage horses, General and Judge. Algonquin was son Archie's calico pony. When Archie was sick in bed with the measles once, his brothers sneaked Algonquin into the White House elevator and up to Archie's bedroom to cheer him up.

Teddy's teenage daughter, Alice, kept a garter snake named Emily Spinach, so named because it was as thin as Alice's Aunt Emily and as green as spinach. Teddy's son Kermit kept a terrier named Blackjack, or Jack for short. Jack was regularly chased by the family cat, Tom Quartz. The family also kept another cat, Slippers (who had six toes), a badger named Josiah, and guinea pigs: Dewey Senior, Dewey Junior, Bob Evans, Bishop Down, and Father O'Grady.

Theodore Roosevelt's children sit for a portrait with family pets in 1901. From left to right: Ethel, Theodore, Alice, Quentin, Kermit, and Archibald. This is a hand-colored reproduction from a black-and-white original photograph.

Quentin Roosevelt, son of President Theodore Roosevelt, rides Algonquin, the pony of his brother Archie, accompanied by a police officer assigned to the White House, circa 1902.

What animals the Roosevelts couldn't house they donated to local zoos, among them a hyena, a wildcat, a lion, a zebra, two parrots, and five bears.

Calvin Coolidge, who collected almost as many pets as Roosevelt, likewise sent several animals off to local zoos, including lion cubs, a bear, a wallaby, and a pygmy hippo. Despite the animals sent packing, Calvin and his wife Grace maintained a small zoo at the White House.

Calvin and Grace showcased their love of dogs with two handsome white collies, Prudence Prim and Rob Roy, and their beloved Paul Pry, an Airedale. So popular was Rob Roy with Grace Coolidge that the dog was included in the official portrait of the first lady. She held the frisky Rob Roy in place for the portrait by feeding him candy.

The Coolidges' other dogs included a pair of chow chows named Tiny Tim and Blackberry, a brown collie named Ruby Rough, a Shetland sheepdog named Calamity Jane, a bulldog named Boston Beans, a yellow collie named Bessie, a bird dog named Palo Alto, a black Belgian shepherd (a Malinois, more commonly known as a police dog) named King Kole, and a fox terrier named Peter Pan.

Like many canine pets in the White House, Peter Pan was untrained, and he often became excited when among visitors to the White House. On one summer day on the White House lawn Peter Pan snapped at the swishing skirt of a woman being entertained as a guest of the first family. The unprovoked attack, in which the dog caught the woman's skirt in his teeth and left her body partially exposed, embarrassed the president and Mrs. Coolidge and earned the snap-happy terrier a banishment from the White House and a trip back to the family home in Massachusetts. There are consequences, and no presidential pardons, for bad behavior.

The Coolidge family parade of pets at the White House went well beyond canines to include two cats named Tiger and Blackie, three canaries named Snowflake,

Nip, and Tuck; a goose, a thrush, a mockingbird, two raccoons named Rebecca and Horace, and a donkey named Ebenezer.

Although the Coolidges did not keep a bobcat named Smoky, who was a gift sent by Tennessee's Great Smoky Mountains Association, they accepted it for compelling political reasons. Smoky was captured in the strongest Republican county in the nation where, in President Coolidge's 1924 election, 442 of 452—98 percent of the vote—went to Silent Cal.

Former President Calvin Coolidge and first lady Grace Coolidge sit with their pet dogs—a black Belgian police dog, King Kole (left) and a white collie, Rob Roy—on the grounds of the then-new Coolidge home in Northampton, Massachusetts, in June 1930.

President Calvin Coolidge and first lady Grace Coolidge with their white collie, Rob Roy, at the White House portico in November 1924.

THE FIRST IKE IN THE WHITE HOUSE

President Woodrow Wilson, distinguished intellectual and former president of Princeton University, appreciated both house and field animals, and in one very visible instance, their symbolism. During World War I President Wilson brought to the White House a flock of sheep and a tobacco-chewing ram named Old Ike to demonstrate to the nation that the White House was conserving manpower and materials in keeping its lawn trimmed. They were the president's pets, but more importantly they were symbols of the president's patriotism.

Thirteen sheep and Old Ike roamed the South Lawn, nibbling not only the White House grass but also the shrubbery and the beds of perennials. The president's patriotic gesture had unleashed an unintended consequence—a "scorched earth" policy of lawn and gardening maintenance! President Wilson had unwittingly sacrificed the White House gardens as his personal contribution to the war effort. When the war ended the president gave the sheep and Old Ike to L. C. Probert, manager of the Washington bureau of the Associated Press, who shipped them to his farm in Maryland.

Old Ike had an addiction to chewing tobacco. The nicotine in the chewing tobacco, which was fed to him by his caretakers, hooked Old Ike early on and continued until he was placed in his grave. When Old Ike didn't get his daily ration in a prompt manner, he unabashedly begged for his tobacco treat—any kind of tobacco. And when he spotted a bit of tobacco, he immediately set out to get it.

According to Margaret Truman's account in her book *White House Pets*, Old Ike and L. C. Probert, who was a cigar smoker, contested Ike's daily fix one day as Probert was mending a fence while holding an unlit cigar in his mouth. Ike approached Probert and communicated his desire for the unlit tobacco by nudging the newsman-turned-farmer several times. Growing annoyed, Probert slapped Ike across his nose, startling the tobacco seeker. But Ike wasn't so easily deterred or dispatched. He waited until Probert's mending chores caused him to bend over. Bam! Old Ike rammed Probert from behind, knocking him to the ground. But the blow did not dislodge the unlit cigar from Probert's mouth. The strong clench by Probert of his cigar taught Old Ike a memorable math lesson: Two butts do not make one chaw.

The legacy of President Wilson's sheep lived beyond his term. Thanks to Ike's prowess with the ewes, Wilson's flock of thirteen sheep grew to seventy. Five years after our twenty-eighth president left office, Probert had the wool from his flock made into blankets, which were given as mementos to friends and former associates of President Wilson, and to current President Calvin Coolidge.

Old Ike died in 1927 with a chaw of tobacco in his mouth, Probert's final treat tendered to the presidency's most famous ram—and its first Ike.

Before he went to Washington and took up residence in the White House, Abraham Lincoln's pets included a variety of four-legged animals—pigs, dogs, cats, and a horse that he needed for transportation in his law practice—but no feathered friends. This changed when he welcomed a turkey named Jack to the White House.

The turkey arrived in the fall of 1863. It was sent courtesy of a friend who intended the turkey to be the first family's Christmas dinner. While the days counted down to the twenty-fifth of December, ten-year old Thomas "Tad" Lincoln, the president's youngest son, and Jack became friends and regular playmates. Jack and Tad went everywhere together.

A short time prior to the holiday, Tad discovered to his horror that Jack, his new pal and playmate, was on the dinner menu. He ran sobbing to his father and pleaded for him to save Jack's life. Lincoln, who always made time for Tad despite his official duties, interrupted an important meeting to write a reprieve for Jack on a card and hand it to his grateful son. Jack was back, the beneficiary of the first and only pardon granted by a president for a Christmas-dinner turkey.

Charlie, Caroline Kennedy's pet Welsh terrier, inspects a turkey presented to President John Kennedy after a traditional Thanksgiving week ceremony at the White House on November 19, 1963. President Kennedy pardoned the bird, sending it back to the farm.

PART 3

NOT A WARTIME MOUNT IN SIGHT, JUST TOP DOGS AND FIRST DOGS
Herbert Hoover (1929–1933) to Barack Obama (2009–   )

The near full century of the presidency from Franklin Delano Roosevelt (1933–1945) to Barack Obama (2009–) has been notable for the ascendancy of the dog as the preferred presidential pet, despite the fact that in recent years there have been fewer dogs per presidential household. Presidents Herbert Hoover, Franklin Delano Roosevelt, John F. Kennedy, and Lyndon B. Johnson had a combined total of thirty-seven dogs (including pups) as presidential pets. Not counting pups, no president since JFK has housed more than three dogs in the White House kennel. Nevertheless, the eighteen acres at 1600 Pennsylvania Avenue have truly gone to the dogs.

Presidents beginning in 1930

Above: *President Franklin D. Roosevelt and first lady Eleanor Roosevelt relax on the lawn of their estate in Hyde Park, New York, with their pet dog, Meggie, in August 1933.* Right: *President Gerald Ford relaxes with his pet dog Liberty while working in the Oval Office on a Sunday afternoon.*

and through Obama's presidency have kept first dogs of various breeds, a fairly even mix of large and small, short-haired and long-haired, stout and lean, hyper and docile. Presidents Ford,

Below: *President Bill Clinton, first lady Hillary Clinton and first puppy Buddy leave the White House in March 1998 for the presidential retreat at Camp David, Maryland.* Right: *President Lyndon Johnson howls with his dog, Yuki, as his grandson Patrick Lyndon Nugent looks on in January 1968.* Opposite: *President Gerald Ford and his daughter Susan play with their new dog Liberty on the grounds of the White House in October 1974. Liberty, named after the spirit of Philadelphia, was the third golden retriever owned by the Ford family. She was given to the president as an eight-month-old puppy by his daughter Susan and White House photographer David Hume Kennerly.*

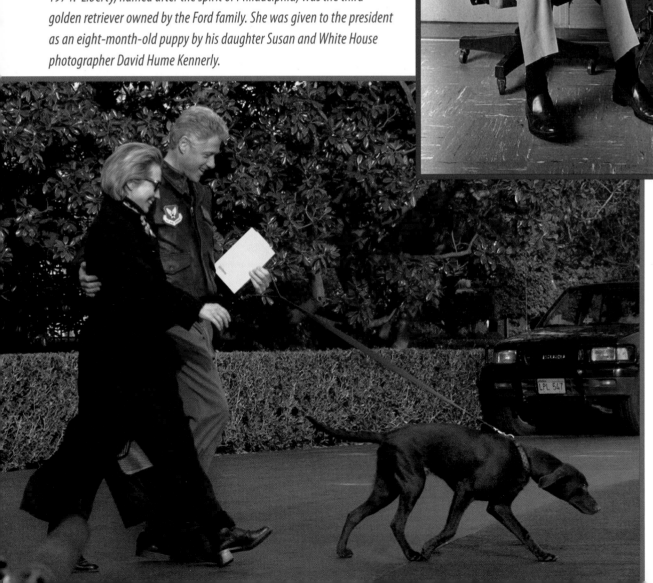

Nixon, Eisenhower, and Clinton preferred large popular breeds, respectively a golden retriever named Liberty, an Irish setter named King Timahoe, a Weimaraner named Heidi, and a chocolate Labrador named Buddy—all breeds used in hunting.

Lyndon Baines Johnson loved hunting dogs too, and the beagle breed that he favored suited his personality. He had two beagles, Him and Her (as well as Yuki, a mutt). Beagles jump-start rabbits in thick underbrush and briar patches, and chase them with their nose and a raucous, throaty blend of yips, barks, and

Below: *First pet beagle Him gets a handshake from President Lyndon Johnson and a pat from first lady Lady Bird Johnson as the president arrives at the White House in October 1965 after a gall bladder and kidney stone operation at Bethesda Naval Hospital. Opposite: Republican presidential candidate Texas Governor George W. Bush and running mate Dick Cheney walk down a dirt road to meet with reporters, accompanied by Bush's dog Spot, near Crawford, Texas, in November, 2000.*

Opposite: *Mufffin, the pet dog of Ronald Reagan and his wife Nancy enjoys the couple's attention at the Reagans' Pacific Palisades, California, home in August 1976.* Above: *Monte Snyder, chauffeur of President Franklin D. Roosevelt, poses with FDR's dogs Meggie the Scotch terrier, left, and Major, the police dog, on the White House grounds in March 1933.*

President George H. W. Bush gestures for his dog, Millie, to return home after she ran to the president's helicopter, Marine One, on the White House lawn in April 1989.

howls. LBJ and one of his dogs often performed a duet, blending their respective on-the-trail howls into a distinctive melody for media covering the White House.

Him and Her stood fifteen inches high, slightly taller than the other small dogs who have undertaken the role of first pet during the late twentieth century. These include the terriers of George W. Bush (Barney), John F. Kennedy (Charlie), and Franklin Delano Roosevelt (Fala); and the spaniels of Harry Truman (Feller), Ronald Reagan (Rex), and George H.W. Bush (Millie). President Reagan loved riding his horse, El Alamein, at Rancho del Cielo in California, but today at the White House it is truly a dog's world, a world of Top Dogs and their canines without a wartime mount—or even a racing filly—in sight.

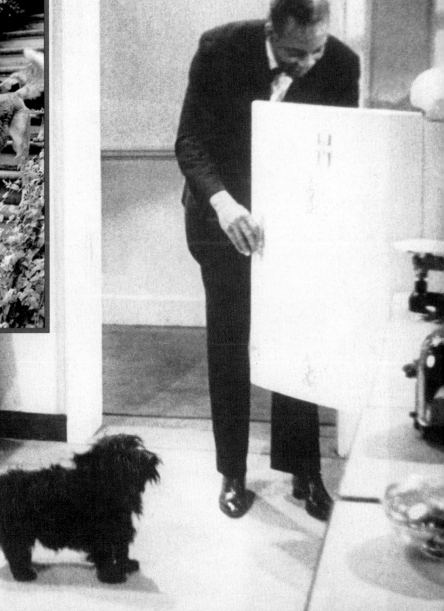

Below: *In a photo from the MGM film* Fala, *President Franklin D. Roosevelt's Scotch terrier Fala waits for a White House staff member to secure his breakfast, a dog biscuit, from the refrigerator. The biscuit was brought on a tray to the president's bedroom along with his master's food.*

Opposite: *King Tut, the German shepherd belonging to President Herbert Hoover, stations himself with a White House guard in April 1929.* Above: *President Herbert Hoover and first lady Lou Henry Hoover and their dogs in the final year of his presidential term.*

First lady Eleanor Roosevelt and President Franklin D. Roosevelt enjoy the afternoon sun at their country home in Hyde Park, New York, in October 1936 with their dog Jack.

31. Herbert Hoover (1929–1933)

Dogs: Police dogs King Tut and Pat, an elkhound named Weeje, fox terriers Big Ben and Sonnie, a Scotch collie named Glen, an Eskimo dog named Yukon, an Irish wolfhound named Patrick, and an Irish setter named Eaglehurst Gillette.

Other: Billy, an opossum.

32. Franklin D. Roosevelt (1933–1945)

Dogs: Fala, a black Scottie, Major, a German shepherd, Meggie, a Scotch terrier, Winks, a Llewellyn setter, Blaze, a mastiff belonging to Elliot Roosevelt, President, a Great Dane, Tiny, an English sheepdog, and two dogs of unknown breed, Pal and Dutchess.

A wheelchair-bound President Franklin D. Roosevelt holds his black Scottie Fala while talking to Ruthie Bie, granddaughter of the caretakers of the Hill Top Cottage at his Hyde Park, New York, home in February 1941. Roosevelt was stricken with polio in August 1921.

Above: President Franklin D. Roosevelt and first lady Eleanor Roosevelt relax at their Hyde Park, New York, home in July 1941 with first dog Fala. Right: President Franklin D. Roosevelt pets Fala, his Scottish terrier, in 1939. Fala's original name was Big Boy, but FDR renamed him Murray the Outlaw of Falahill after John Murray of Falahill, a famous Scottish ancestor. FDR later shortened the name to Fala.

33. Harry S. Truman (1945–1953)

Dogs: Mike, an Irish setter belonging to daughter Margaret, Feller, a cocker spaniel,

Other: Mike the Magicat, Dewey's Goat, named after Truman's 1948 presidential opponent, Thomas E. Dewey.

34. Dwight D. Eisenhower (1953–1961)

Dogs: Heidi, a Weimaraner, and Spunky, a black Scottie.

35. John F. Kennedy (1961–1963)

Dogs: Clipper, a German shepherd, Shannon, an Irish cocker spaniel, Wolf, an Irish

Above: *President John F. Kennedy examines a salamander named Shadrach as nephew Robert Kennedy, Jr., 7, watches. The salamander was a gift from Robert to the president. Opposite: The family of President John F. Kennedy vacations with their first dogs and puppies in this undated photo. From left: Caroline, first lady Jacqueline Kennedy, John Jr. and President Kennedy.*

wolfhound, Charlie, a Welsh terrier belonging to daughter Caroline, Pushinka, an unknown breed that was a gift to Caroline from Soviet Premier Nikita Khrushchev, and Charlie's four "pupniks" by Pushinka: Butterfly, White Tips, Blackie, and Streaker.

Horses: Sardar, belonging to first lady Jacqueline Kennedy, a gift from the president of Pakistan.

Other: Macaroni, a pony belonging to daughter Caroline, Leprechaun, a pony belonging to son John, Jr., and another pony named Tex, a rabbit named Zsa Zsa, a canary named Robin, parakeets named Bluebelle and Maybelle, hamsters named Billie and Debbie, a Guinea pig, and Irish deer.

Above: *President John F. Kennedy's daughter Caroline Kennedy rides her pony, Macaroni, on the south grounds of the White House in March 1962.* Above right: *Macaroni enjoys a treat.* Opposite: *First lady Jacqueline Kennedy rides with son John, Jr., 2, on Sardar, her gift from President Ayub Khan of Pakistan, while daughter Caroline, 5, accompanies her on her pony Macaroni in November 1962 on Kennedy's Glen Ora estate near Middleburg, Virginia.*

DID YOU KNOW?
JFK's Welsh terrier named Charlie was a nephew to the dog that played the role of Asta in the classic movie **The Thin Man.**

36. Lyndon B. Johnson (1963–1969)

Dogs: Yuki, a mongrel, Old Beagle and pups Kim, Freckles, Dumpling, Little Chap, beagles Him and Her, Blanco, a white collie, Edgar, an unknown breed that was a gift from J. Edgar Hoover.

Other: Hamsters and lovebirds.

DID YOU KNOW? Him and Her, the two beagles of Lyndon B. Johnson made the cover of the June 19, 1964 issue of Life magazine.

Opposite: Him and Her, the beagles of President Lyndon B. Johnson, rest on the grounds of the White House in October 1964. Below: Blanco, the white collie of president Lyndon B. Johnson, shares the Oval Office with the president just prior to his gall bladder operation in October 1965.

Opposite: *President Lyndon B. Johnson and his family gather before the Christmas tree on December 24, 1968.* Left: *President Johnson proves he's a pretty good cowhand as he puts his horse, Lady B, through the paces of rounding up a Hereford yearling on his LBJ Ranch near Stonewall, Texas, in November 1964.* Below: *President Johnson confers with a delegation of the nation's governors in his White House office in March 1966 while one of his beagles, far right, checks out activities on the White House lawn.*

37. Richard Nixon (1969–1974)

Dogs: Checkers, his cocker spaniel while vice president, Vicky, a French poodle belonging to daughter Julie, Pasha, a Yorkshire terrier belonging to daughter Tricia, and King Timahoe, an Irish setter.

Other: Fish.

38. Gerald Ford (1974–1977)

Dogs: Liberty, a golden retriever who had eight pups

Senator Richard Nixon, Republican vice-presidential candidate, relaxes with his wife Pat, their children Julie and Patricia, and their cocker spaniel Checkers on the lawn of their home in Washington, D.C., in September 1952 following the "Checkers" speech.

President Gerald Ford, first lady Betty Ford and their daughter Susan admire their golden retriever Liberty and her litter of nine puppies in September 1975 at the White House.

while at the White House and who later became a guide dog for the blind.

Other: Chan, a Siamese cat, and Flag, a deer.

Left: *Liberty dropped by while President Ford was meeting with Secretary of State Henry Kissinger and Major General Brent Scowcroft, deputy assistant for national security affairs.* Below: *Liberty, President Gerald Ford's golden retriever, receives greetings from the president as he makes an unexpected visit to the Oval Office in November 1974.*

President Gerald Ford and first lady Betty Ford pose with family members and their dog at the White House in 1975.

39. Jimmy Carter (1977–1981)

Dogs: Grits, a mutt.

Other: Misty Milarky Ying Yang, a Siamese cat who didn't get along with Grits.

Below: *While boating on a small pond near Plains, Georgia in April 1979, President Jimmy Carter uses an oar to splash water at a rabbit which swam near his boat. The president was later kidded about the "killer rabbit" episode.* Right: *Georgia Governor Jimmy Carter and his daughter Amy, 7, take a look at her pet hamster Sleepy before packing up his cage in the process of moving out of the Governor's Mansion in December 1974.*

40. Ronald Reagan (1981–1989)

Dogs: Rex, a King Charles spaniel; Lucky, a Bouvier des Flandres (sheepdog) who proved too big and rambunctious to handle (after being sent to Reagan's ranch he was replaced by Rex).

Other: Horses and dogs at the ranch, and a goldfish.

Left: *Nancy Reagan, wife of Republican presidential candidate Ronald Reagan, pets a horse on their ranch near Santa Barbara, California, in June 1980.*
Below: *President Ronald Reagan and first lady Nancy Reagan walk with their dog Rex on the grounds of the White House after they returned by helicopter from Camp David, Maryland.*

Above: *First lady Nancy Reagan cradles an early Christmas present, a King Charles spaniel, as she and President Reagan stroll along the grounds of the White House in December 1985 after returning from New York. The new dog, a brother of a dog owned by* National Review *editor William Buckley Jr., is described as "housebroken and extremely well-mannered." Opposite: President George H. W. Bush is followed by his dog Millie across the grounds of the White House in December 1992.*

41. George H. W. Bush (1989–1993)

Dogs: Millie, a Springer spaniel who wrote a best-selling book (with the help of first lady Barbara Bush), and Ranger, one of Millie's pups.

Left: *First lady Barbara Bush pets the family dogs Millie, bottom, and Ranger on the steps of the White House in April 1991.* Above: *President George H. W. Bush is chased by granddaughter Marshall Bush and dog Ranger, an offspring of Millie, in May 1990.* Right: *President George H. W. Bush holds one of first dog Millie's six puppies in March 1989. First lady Barbara Bush served as midwife for the birth of Millie's puppies.*

Left: *Chelsea Clinton pets outgoing first dog Millie as President George H.W. Bush, first lady Barbara Bush and President-elect Bill Clinton look on at the White House, January 20, 1993. The Clinton family went to the White House to pick up the Bushes, escorting them to Capitol Hill and Clinton's presidential swearing-in ceremony.*

Left: *President Bill Clinton returns to the White House from Camp David, Maryland, with his dog Buddy in March 1999. Above: First lady Hillary Rodham Clinton looks on as President Clinton holds Socks, the Clintons' cat, who is petted by a Washington area elementary school student in the State Dining Room of the White House in December 1993. The president and Mrs. Clinton hosted the students with the president reading "The Night Before Christmas."*

42. Bill Clinton (1993–2001)

Dogs: Buddy, a chocolate Labrador.

Other: Socks, a cat.

President Bill Clinton, his daughter Chelsea, center, and wife Hillary walk toward a helicopter with their Labrador retriever Buddy as they depart the White House for a vacation in Martha's Vineyard, Massachusetts, on Aug. 18, 1998. This 1999 Pulitzer Prize–winning photo by the Associated Press was taken the day after President Clinton gave a nationally televised statement admitting his relationship with White House intern Monica Lewinsky was "not appropriate."

43. George W. Bush (2001–2009)

Dogs: Spot, a Springer spaniel (Millie's puppy), Barney, a black Scottish terrier, Miss Beazley, a black Scottish terrier.

Other: Ofelia, a Texas long-horn steer, India and Ernie, cats.

President George W. Bush and first lady Laura Bush show off their new puppy Miss Beazley, a Scottish terrier, in January 2005, on the grounds of the White House. The puppy was a birthday gift to the first lady from President Bush. The dog was nicknamed Beazley-Weazley.

Below: *President George W. Bush carries his two dogs, Barney, foreground, and Miss Beazley, background, down the steps of Air Force One upon his arrival in Washington from Texas in August 2006.*

Opposite: *With first lady Laura Bush by his side, President George W. Bush shows off a new rug designed for the Oval Office being enjoyed by their English Springer spaniel Spot during an end-of-the-year meeting with reporters at the White House in December 2001. Above: President George W. Bush and first lady Laura Bush stand with their dogs Spot, left, and Barney, right, after their arrival in Waco, Texas, in November 2001.*

44. Barack Obama
   ## (2009–   )

Dogs: Bo (Diddley), a Portuguese water dog that was a gift from the late Senator Ted Kennedy.

Below: *President Barack Obama's daughters Malia, left and Sasha, right, play with their dog Bo during a visit to the Children's National Medical Center in Washington, in December 2009. Right: President Obama's family dog, Bo, stands near the West Wing of the White House in December 2009.*

Malia Obama walks with their new dog Bo as President Barack Obama, first lady Michelle Obama and Sasha follow on the grounds of the White House in April 2009. Bo was first named Charlie by his original owners and he is officially registered with the American Kennel Club as Amigo's New Hope. The Obama children named him Bo in honor of their cousin's cat of the same name.

Above: *President Barack Obama, first lady Michelle Obama, and daughters Malia and Sasha, walk with their six-month-old Portuguese water dog Bo on the White House grounds, Tuesday, April 14, 2009, the day of Bo's official debut. The breed fulfilled the Obama family's need for a pet with a hypoallergenic coat. Right: President Barack Obama hugs his daughters Sasha, left, Malia, right, and dog Bo as he arrives on the White House grounds in September 2009.*

Poodle

Wheaten
Terrier

Bichon
Frisé

Chinese
Crested

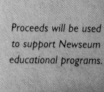

*Proceeds will be used
to support Newseum
educational programs.*

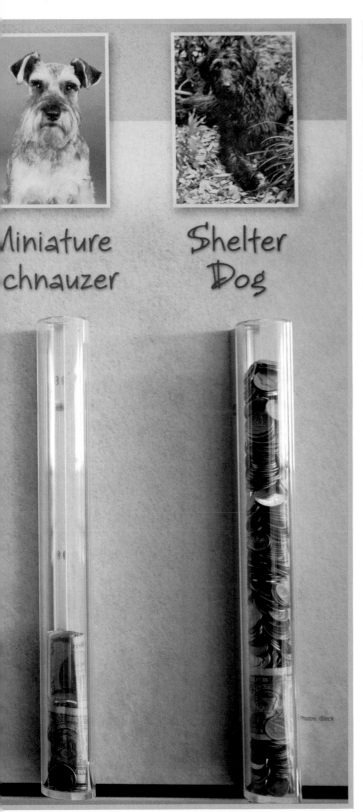

Miniature
chnauzer

Shelter
Dog

Photos: iStock

Left: *In a poll sponsored as part of an exhibit, "First Dogs: American Presidents and Their Pets," in November 2008 at the Newseum in Washington, D.C., the popular vote favored a shelter dog for the Obamas. The poll consisted of participants dropping money into a tube to show their choice for the next presidential pet. The Obamas chose a Portuguese water dog named Bo. Right: This is the official White House portrait of the Obama family dog Bo, a Portuguese water dog, on the South Lawn of the White House.*

The White House has been home to just one best-selling presidetial pet: President George H.W. Bush's Springer spaniel Millie, who wrote *Millie's Book—As Dictated to Barbara Bush*. Published in fall of 1990, Millie's Book rocketed up the *New York Times* and *Washington Post* bestseller lists by Thanksgiving, passing former President Ronald Reagan's memoir, *An American Life*, on the lists (at number three on the Times list, it was five notches above the Reagan book). *Millie's Book* even outsold President Bush's quasi-memoir, *All the Best, George Bush: My Life in Letters and Other Writings*, which was published in 2000. Sales of the book raised nearly one million dollars for Barbara Bush's campaign for literacy, and it showed the Bush family as attentive, appreciative caretakers of their first pet.

In the book, Millie described the everyday life at the White House, everything from hunting on the grounds for squirrels and other small prey to participation in the morning briefings of the president. As one reader enthused, the book's inside peeks at the president's daily routine and his personal family life "made the Bush family seem just like everyday folks who are just like the rest of us." *Millie's Book* with Millie's musings and frontline reports of the first family's goings on had struck an appealing chord among Americans.

When Americans view their presidents they see powerful individuals who have enormous responsibilities, duties, and powers. When they see their presidents interacting with their pets they glimpse the personal and playful side of their leaders. The nation's first pets carry out, in a truly nonpartisan fashion and more effectively than any other communications vehicle, the task of revealing the character and illuminating the personalities of the president and members of the first family. Thus, they allow the entire citizenry to celebrate the universal bonds and rewards of pet ownership—caring, friendship, fidelity, and loyalty—that are forged between a pet and its master or caretaker.

Historians note that President Bush genuinely loved Millie. Millie was always present when the president's helicopter arrived. President Bush always showed his delight by greeting Millie first. Bush also installed especially for Millie a dog biscuit dispenser—a replica of a gumball machine—at Camp David. Millie and the president even showered together.

Before leaving the White House in 1993 (Millie was a one-term first pet), she gave birth to six pups. Her daughter, Fetcher Spot Bush, more commonly known as Spot, returned to the White House as the first pet of President George W. Bush, son of

Millie's master. In 1992, Pickard China issued the first presidential dog bowl, aptly named "Millie's Bowl," commemorating the distinguished first pet and best-selling author. The bowl featured a twenty-four-karat gold inlaid presidential seal, a gold and cobalt blue border and a gold inscription: *Millie*.

Millie died in 1997 at age twelve of a sudden illness at President Bush's summer home in Kennebunkport, Maine.

Below: *First lady Barbara Bush and granddaughter Marshall Lloyd Bush visit with first dog Millie and her six puppies at the White House in March 1989, one day after Mille gave birth.* Right: *Millie walks across the White House grounds with the president and first lady after returning from a holiday weekend in Kennebunkport, Maine.*

FDR'S BELOVED FALA
THE MOST FAMOUS OF ALL WHITE HOUSE PETS

The most famous of all White House pets was Fala, a black Scottie, who was one of nine canines with President Franklin Delano Roosevelt during his twelve years and one month at 1600 Pennsylvania Avenue. FDR had a bull mastiff, a Llewellyn setter, a German shepherd, a Great Dane, a sheepdog, two Scotch terriers, Meggie and Fala, and two unknown breeds.

Fala was truly a companion to our thirty-second president, and Roosevelt liked having his first pet with him immensely. Fala attended the president's cabinet meetings and press conferences, plopping down alongside the president's feet. Fala traveled with Roosevelt to international meetings, such as when FDR and Winston Churchill signed the Atlantic Charter aboard the USS *Augusta*. On that occasion, Fala was joined by Rufus, Churchill's poodle.

Fala's role in public affairs included fund-raising during World War II. When the White House launched a campaign to raise funds for the war effort, Fala became an honorary army private. He was awarded the military rank in exchange for a contribution of one dollar. When this quid pro quo fund-raiser was announced, hundreds of thousands of dogs

President Franklin D. Roosevelt steps out to a black-tie affair with pet dog Fala in an undated photograph.

(and their owners) across the nation signed up.

In the election campaign of 1944, the high public visibility and celebrity status of Fala presented a sure-fire opportunity to the opposing Republican Party to attack the president—or so they thought. The dust-up began when an operative started a false rumor that after Fala had been left behind on an island off Alaska during a presidential visit, FDR dispatched a U.S. Navy warship to retrieve his Scottie. They alleged that FDR had squandered and misused public resources.

FDR slipped this campaign trickster's noose during a national radio broadcast when he answered the charges with a clever, tongue-in-cheek explanation: "Republican leaders have not been content with attacks on me, or my wife, or my sons. No, not content with that, they now include my little dog, Fala. Well, of course, I don't resent attacks and

President Franklin D. Roosevelt and first lady Eleanor Roosevelt watch as Fala, their black Scottie, hops onto the jump seat as they leave town hall in Hyde Park, New York, on Nov. 4, 1941. President Roosevelt had just finished voting. Seated next to the first lady in the backseat is Princess Juliana of the Netherlands.

my family doesn't resent attacks, but Fala does resent them. You know, Fala is Scotch, and being a Scottie, as soon as he learned that the Republican fiction writers had concocted a story that I had left him behind on the Aleutian Islands and had sent a destroyer back to find him—at a cost to the taxpayers of two or three or eight or twenty million dollars—his Scotch soul was furious. He has not been the same dog since."

Fala was with FDR when the president died on April 12, 1945. He had accompanied the president on his forty first-visit to Warm Springs, Georgia, where FDR had built a Little White House, a six-room cottage tucked among the rolling hills south of Atlanta. Roosevelt had been drawn to Warm Springs in 1924, seeking a cure for the infantile paralysis that afflicted him. Swimming in the warm mineral water that maintained an average daily temperature of eighty-three degrees and flowed naturally from Pine Mountain gave FDR some limited improvement in his mobility. In the afternoon on this early spring day, Roosevelt, not feeling well, retired to bed.

According to the account of Stanley Coren in his book *The Pawprints of History: Dogs and the Course of Human Events*, Fala, who was lying on the floor in Roosevelt's bedroom, sensed something was amiss with his master and became extremely agitated. "At 3:35 PM, Fala suddenly jumped up and started in the direction of his master. He gave a yip and a whimper and turned around quickly. He acted as if he was looking at something—following something—that was not visible to the human eye. Whimpering plaintively he raced across the floor, his eyes fixed on something in the air. The little black dog charged out of the room, down the short passageway and, with his eyes still pointed skyward, he crashed into the screen door. At that same moment, the doctor pronounced that the president was dead."

Fala's last trip with the president was riding alongside the first lady, Eleanor Roosevelt, in the funeral cortège. FDR was buried in the rose garden of the president's estate in Hyde Park, New York. And when Fala died a few years later, he was buried next to his master, as the president wished.

Acknowledgments

Several people contributed to the creation, development and publishing of this book, and to them we say, "Thanks."

★ Staff of the Associated Press
★ John Monteleone, Andrew Monteleone, Rich Klin and Chuck Michaels of Mountain Lion, Inc.
★ The following photographers:
(l,r,t,b=left, right, top, bottom)

Haraz N. Ghanbari/AP: Front Cover

Marcy Nighswander/AP: Pages 1, 85(r), 123(t)

Gerald Herbert/AP: Pages 2-3, 117, 119, 126

J. Scott Applewhite/AP: Pages 7(r), 22, 80(b), 108(r), 114, Back Cover(Bush(2))

Alex Brandon/AP: Pages 8, 45, 116(r)

Barry Thumma/AP: Page 13

Charles Dharapak/AP: Pages 14-15, 29, 118

Greg Gibson/AP: Page 17(l&r)

Susan Walsh/AP: Pages 18, 24

Doug Mills/AP: Pages 19, 44, 107, 110

Wilfredo Lee/AP: Page 23

William J. Smith/AP: Page 25(l)

Ron Edmonds/AP: Pages 25(r), 109, 111(l), 113, Back Cover(Obama)

Charles P. Gorry/AP: Page 27(r)

Murray Becker/AP: Page 30

Wally Fong/AP: Page 31

Pablo Martinez Monsivais/AP: Page 33

John Rous/AP: Page 41

Eric Draper/AP: Page 83

Walter Zeboski/AP: Pages 84, 105(t)

Bill Hudson/AP: Page 99(t)

Charles Tasnadi/AP: Page 102(b)

Dennis Cook/AP: Pages 105(b), 106

Joe Holloway, Jr./AP: Page 104(t)

Joe Marquette/AP: Page 111(r)

Roberto Borea/AP: Page 112

Eric Gay/AP: Page 115(l)

Evan Vucci/AP: Page 115(r)

Manuel Balce Ceneta/AP: Page 116(l)

Jacquelyn Martin/AP: Page 120

Bob Daugherty/AP: Page 128

Bob Strong/AP: Page 108(l)

White House Photo via AP: Pages 4, 26(l), 26-27, 79, 101, 123(b), Back Cover(LBJ)

Barbara Kinney/White House Photo via AP: Page 356

Paul Morse/White House Photo via AP: Page 36(t)

Eric Draper/White House Photo via AP: Page 37

Yoichi Okamoto/White House Photo via AP: Page 80(t)

Frank Wolfe/White House Photo via AP: Page 98

David Hume Kennerly/White House Photo via AP: Page 102(t)

Chuck Kennedy/White House Photo via AP: Page 121

Margaret Suckley/FDR Presidential Library/National Archives via AP: Page 89

Howard Allen for the White House via AP: Page 95

U.S. Army via AP: Page 43

North Wind Picture Archives via AP: Page 73

Library of Congress via AP: Pages 6-7, 9, 16, 21, 38, 54, 55, 57, 58(l&r), 59, 60, 61, 63(r), 64, 68, 69, 70, 71, 74, 86

AP Photo Collection: Pages 10, 11, 12, 28, 32, 34(l&r), 36(b), 39, 40, 42(l&r), 47, 48-49, 56, 62, 63(l), 65, 67, 75(l&r), 77, 78, 81, 82, 85(l), 87(l&r), 88, 90, 91, 92, 92-93, 94(l&r), 96, 97, 99(b), 100, 103, 104(b), 124, 125

AP Photos are available at *www.apimages.com*

Illustration on p. 51 by Len Ebert

Illustration on p. 52 by Bob Antler

A Marine guard salutes as President George W. Bush's dog Barney disembarks from Marine One on the south lawn of the White House in March 2004 upon his return from Camp David with President Bush and first lady Laura Bush.

From an upstairs window of the White House, first lady Nancy Reagan and Rex, her King Charles spaniel, watch President Ronald Reagan as he conducts the German-American Day ceremony in the Rose Garden in October 1987.